LONDON 20

THE CITY AT A GLANC

C000244878

Barbican
Residential towers are built aro
arts centre in this modernist ci
See p071

St Paul's Cathedral
The once-unmissable landmark is slowly being
overshadowed by nearby developments.
St Paul's Churchyard, EC4, T 7246 8350

Millennium Bridge
Due to early teething problems when the
rush-hour stomp caused it to vibrate, Norman
Foster's span is dubbed the 'wobbly bridge'.

Bank of England
Nikolaus Pevsner called Sir Herbert Baker's
1925-39 near-obliteration of Sir John Soane's
building a 'great architectural crime'.
Threadneedle Street, EC2

Tower 42
Despite being rebranded, reclad and tarted
up, Richard Seifert's 1980 monolith is still
known as the NatWest Tower by most locals.
25 Old Broad Street, EC2

Tate Modern
This vast modern-art museum is housed in
Sir Giles Gilbert Scott's former power station.
See p010

30 St Mary Axe
The profile of this early noughties addition
to the City led to its nickname, the 'Gherkin'.
See p012

Shakespeare's Globe
A 1997 recreation of the theatre demolished
in 1644, the Globe is the brainchild of the
American actor Sam Wanamaker.
21 New Globe Walk, SE1

INTRODUCTION
THE CHANGING FACE OF THE URBAN SCENE

Twenty years ago, London's claim to be one of the world's greatest cities was unconvincing. Now it is perhaps *the* global city. Every talented son or daughter of Europe and beyond, it seems, tries their luck here, seeing if they can make it fly. Many of them man the incredible restaurants, bars, cafés and shops that London offers. From establishment-cool Notting Hill to alternative-cool Hackney, you're as likely to hear Spanish, French or Polish as English.

However, for all its luxurious fixtures and fittings, London is not always easy to enjoy. It is tough and sprawling and inscrutable, violently fluid and fickle. It is full of cliques and protected spaces, of neighbourhoods entirely at odds with one another. But if the recession has dampened the capital's good-times vibe, it hasn't dampened it much. Regeneration is still happening apace. And just as the city's focal point shifted eastwards (a pull accelerated by the 2012 Olympics), the South-East became the site of major redevelopment led by Renzo Piano's Shard (see p067). This is not a city that stands still, and in King's Cross and the Queen Elizabeth Olympic Park, major new districts are being created from scratch. Their aim is to be London, but better. We will see.

Today, the problem is plotting a course through it all, as London scatters its treasures far and wide, and farther and wider. We can think of no other city in the world that requires so much insider nous to navigate properly. And that is where we come in, of course.

ESSENTIAL INFO
FACTS, FIGURES AND USEFUL ADDRESSES

TOURIST OFFICE
Visit London
King's Cross Western Ticket Hall
Euston Road, N1
T 0870 156 6366
www.visitlondon.com

TRANSPORT
Bicycles
www.tfl.gov.uk
Bikes can be hired from docking
stations across central London; there
is no charge for the first 30 minutes
Car hire
Avis
T 0844 581 0147
Hertz
T 0843 309 3078
Public transport
www.tfl.gov.uk
Tube trains run from approximately
5.30am to 12.30am, Monday to Saturday;
6.30am to 12am on Sundays
Taxis
London Black Cabs
T 0795 769 6673

EMERGENCY SERVICES
Emergencies
T 999
Police (non-emergencies)
T 7437 1212
24-hour pharmacy
Zafash
233-235 Old Brompton Road, SW5
T 7373 2798

EMBASSY
US Embassy
24 Grosvenor Square, W1
T 7499 9000
london.usembassy.gov

POSTAL SERVICES
Post office
1 Broadway, SW1
T 0845 722 3344
Shipping
UPS
T 0845 787 7877

BOOKS
London Architecture
by Marianne Butler (Metro Publications)
The London Blue Plaque Guide
by Nick Rennison (The History Press)

WEBSITES
Art
www.ica.org.uk
Design
www.designmuseum.org
Newspaper
www.standard.co.uk

EVENTS
Frieze Art Fair
www.friezelondon.com
100% Design
www.100percentdesign.co.uk
Open House London
www.londonopenhouse.org

COST OF LIVING
**Taxi from Heathrow Airport
to city centre**
£55
Cappuccino
£2.50
Packet of cigarettes
£7.50
Daily newspaper
£1.20
Bottle of champagne
£70

LONDON
Population
8.2 million
Currency
Pound sterling
Telephone codes
United Kingdom: 44
London: 020
Local time
GMT

Oslo

Glasgow   Edinburgh

Copenhagen

Dublin   **UNITED KINGDOM**

Hamburg

Berlin

London

Brussels

AVERAGE TEMPERATURE / °C

40

30

20

10

00

-10

-20

J F M A M J J A S O N D

AVERAGE RAINFALL / MM

120

100

080

060

040

020

000

J F M A M J J A S O N D

NEIGHBOURHOODS

THE AREAS YOU NEED TO KNOW AND WHY

To help you navigate the city, we've chosen the most interesting districts (see below and the map inside the back cover) and colour-coded our featured venues, according to their location; those venues that are outside these areas are not coloured.

CENTRAL

London's West End is really the centre of the modern city. Bloomsbury, spiritual home of the literati, is a kind of oasis, as is Marylebone, which is now a chichi shopping destination. Soho has lost steam to Shoreditch as a nocturnal playground, but you'll still find the grandest hotels in Mayfair, including Claridge's (see p025).

NORTH

Traditionally, the hills of north London have had a more bohemian air than the West. Primrose Hill is one of the city's most desirable enclaves, Camden gets crammed with tourists, and King's Cross is undergoing an ambitious urban overhaul, with St Pancras station as its focal point.

THE CITY

This is the world's biggest financial centre, and the huge wages of the 'City boys' spill west into the top clubs and restaurants. The area is a mix of shining towers, cranes and Victorian pubs, which are largely deserted at night, although the lack of residents is now attracting hip nightspots.

SOUTH-WEST

Purest posh, this district has some of the most expensive property on the planet. You can't move for lords, ladies, oil-funded Arab royalty, Russian oligarchs and the odd Hollywood A-lister. It also houses a number of London's finest restaurants, such as Dinner by Heston Blumenthal (see p048).

WEST

Notting Hill can feel like a fantasy land, with its pristine stucco townhouses, chic boutiques and eateries, including Dock Kitchen (see p042), and the famous and picturesque Portobello street market. The sheer pleasantness of it all can unnerve some, although visitors may believe they have found an urban idyll.

WESTMINSTER

Britain's administrative heart is the site of royal palaces and was once the seat of a globe-spanning empire. It is the country's ancient and wheezing engine room. Our tip is to visit Tate Britain (Millbank, SW1, T 7887 8888), then take a river boat to the South Bank for the most splendid of views.

EAST

After a transformation, this area dragged the epicentre of London cool sharply eastwards. In Clerkenwell, designers, architects and commercial creatives live, work and eat at venues such as Morito (see p057) and Workshop Coffee Co (27 Clerkenwell Road, EC1, T 7253 5754).

SOUTH-EAST

The opening of Tate Modern (see p011) in 2000 forced Londoners to accept that Bankside was worth a look. Borough Market (Southwark Street, SE1, T 7407 1002) draws foodies, and evidence of Bermondsey's regeneration comes in the form of the White Cube gallery (see p036).

LANDMARKS

THE SHAPE OF THE CITY SKYLINE

It's hard to imagine now, but 50 years ago a portrait of the London skyline was a celebration of the smaller, gentler things in life. Quaintness was the city's stock-in-trade. Until the early 1960s, the height of new buildings was prescribed, not by some far-reaching architectural masterplan but by how high a fireman's ladder could reach – about 30m, as it happened. Inevitably, it all changed later in the decade. The BT Tower (see p014), looking like a *2001: A Space Odyssey* film set *avant la lettre*, seemed to be a manifestation of an altogether better future. Today, Foster + Partners' 30 St Mary Axe (see p012) is a similarly iconic presence – it appears to be the final destination at the end of every major street, like one of the large buddhas in Bangkok. But its status as London's totemic tower has now been taken by Renzo Piano's jaw-dropper of a glass pyramid, The Shard (see p067), just south of the Thames near London Bridge station. It's impossible to ignore and hard to resist.

Trellick Tower (see p015) is a reference point in west London, and was equally controversial (JG Ballard allegedly based his novel *High-Rise*, in which tenants begin floor-on-floor warfare, on this block). Ernö Goldfinger's landmark has become a cult item, featured in pop songs and on T-shirts. His tower is now desirable real estate, the defining icon of modernism's rehabilitation and of the city's acceptance of its radically changing face.

For full addresses, see Resources.

Tate Modern

When Swiss architects Herzog & de Meuron created a sister gallery to Tate Britain (see p032), in a former power station in South-East London, it seemed madness. Today, Tate Modern is a poster child for the regenerative power of architecture, yet the rawness of Sir Giles Gilbert Scott's building remains the real point. An extension, part of which is open (see p034), is underway.
Bankside, SE1, T 7887 8888

30 St Mary Axe

Completed in 2003, Foster + Partners' 'Gherkin' or, more properly, 30 St Mary Axe, dominates the City skyline – for now. Actually designed by Norman Foster's former chief lieutenant, Ken Shuttleworth (the man behind Hong Kong's Chek Lap Kok Airport), the Gherkin swells at its mid-point and tapers to a glass dome, which houses one of the world's most covetable staff canteens, part of which has been reopened as a members' bar. Its cigar shape means that the public spaces at the base are not blighted by the street-level hurricanes that traditional towers produce. Inside, it is divided into a series of coiling atriums and gardens, which work to open up the building and link the 40 floors, which are far more than a series of stacked shelves for worker ants. *30 St Mary Axe, EC3*

Centre Point

Richard Seifert's influence on the London cityscape is unmatched (cast an eye over his 1962 Space House at 1 Kemble Street, WC2), but not always in a good way. When this office development was unveiled in 1966, it was the tallest building in London. It was also, famously, one of the most underutilised. The developer, Harry Hyams, wanted to rent the whole building to a single tenant and, as a result, it stood empty for many years. Schemes to turn it into housing have been mooted over the decades, but it seems that its legacy will be as a pointer to shoppers on Oxford Street, and to the power of the property developer's greed. On the top floors, the Paramount restaurant (T 7420 2900), and Tom Dixon-designed bar offer one of the most dramatic panoramas in the city.
101-103 New Oxford Street, WC1

BT Tower

Unusually for an instantly recognisable landmark, during the first 30 years of its existence the BT Tower (formerly known as the Post Office Tower) did not appear on any maps. As a microwave relay station for the national phone company – fabulously exotic technology for the time – it was an unlikely inclusion in the Official Secrets Act, and surely the only one with a revolving restaurant on top. But then, ever since it was officially opened in 1966 by a noted left-wing politician (Tony Benn) and the owner of a chain of holiday camps (Billy Butlin), the tower has always been a mix of contradictions. The restaurant was bombed by the IRA in 1971 and was closed in 1980, although occasionally it's used for corporate events. As a telecoms tower, the building is still in operational use.
60 Cleveland Street, W1

Trellick Tower

Ernö Goldfinger's high-rise looms over the stuccoed townhouses and chichi eateries of Ladbroke Grove, a last blast of top-quality brutalism in the UK. The architect started work on the 31-storey structure in 1968 and it was completed in 1972. The look of Trellick Tower is of a monumental concrete slab with add-ons. It is defined by a separate service tower connected to the 'living units' in the main building by concealed walkways every third floor, with a cantilevered boiler house hanging above it. The apartments themselves are huge, for social housing, and have large windows and balconies. Goldfinger took obsessive care of the details. The balconies have cedar cladding, and the windows are double-glazed and spin round for ease of cleaning.

5 Golborne Road, W10

HOTELS

WHERE TO STAY AND WHICH ROOMS TO BOOK

In <u>The Savoy</u> (opposite), <u>Claridge's</u> (see p025) and <u>The Dorchester</u> (Park Lane, W1, T 7629 8888), London has some of the world's most famous hotels – landlocked Titanics, all huge ballrooms and gilded doormen. The <u>Corinthia</u> (Whitehall Place, SW1, T 7930 8181), unveiled in 2011, is a contemporary take on the grand pile, while <u>Café Royal</u> (see p026), a more demi-monde destination, has been rethought by David Chipperfield. The city also claims various appealing townhouse operations (see p024); top-quality one-offs, such as <u>The Zetter</u> (86-88 Clerkenwell Road, EC1, T 7324 4444); and, in the Firmdale empire (see p029), a uniquely British boutique movement. Terence Conran's <u>Boundary</u> (see p030) helped make Shoreditch's Redchurch Street a fashionable strip, and, further east, <u>Town Hall Hotel & Apartments</u> (Patriot Square, E2, T 7871 0460) is a beautifully executed midcentury fantasy.

And the London hotel scene is about to get even hotter. David Collins is transforming the 1922 Port of London Authority Building into <u>10 Trinity Square</u> (EC3), André Balazs is looking to launch in Marylebone, and Tom Dixon is due to turn part of the South Bank's pomo-ish monster <u>Sea Containers House</u> (SE1) into a Morgans hotel. In 2013, the Shangri-La group opens its segment of <u>The Shard</u> (see p067), while restaurant giants Chris Corbin and Jeremy King are planning a Mayfair establishment for 2014. *For full addresses and room rates, see Resources.*

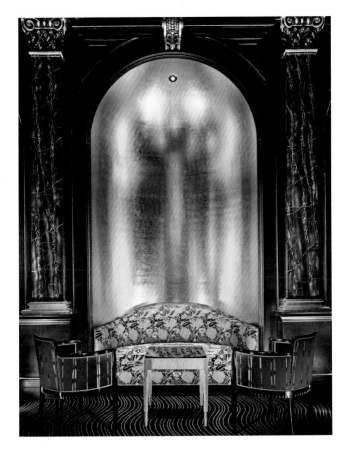

The Savoy

The renovation of this most iconic hotel (it was once run by César Ritz, with Auguste Escoffier in the kitchen) involved a £220m, three-year overhaul – surely no easy task. But interior designer Pierre-Yves Rochon and Pentagram's John Rushworth, who were charged with dusting off the Savoy's 'identity', did a respectful job, placing an emphasis on fine materials and drama only where it was needed. The hotel's cluster of restaurants includes Gordon Ramsay's Savoy Grill (T 7592 1600), and the River Restaurant (T 7420 2111), which is run by the Canadian-born chef James Pare. The gilt-edged Beaufort Bar (above) sits on the former cabaret stage where Gershwin once performed *Rhapsody in Blue*, and, of course, there's the American Bar. *Strand, WC2, T 7836 4343, www.fairmont.com/savoy*

St Pancras Renaissance
After a long refurbishment, Sir George Gilbert Scott's Midland Grand hotel at St Pancras reopened in 2011. Much of the decor is calmly contemporary, yet mindful of original details, as in the Chambers Junior Suite (pictured). One of the finest staircases in Europe and the ladies' (no) smoking room have been restored to their Gothic glory.
Euston Road, NW1, T 7841 3540

Bulgari

London's sparkling addition to the Bulgari chain, set in a sombre Portland-stone block in Knightsbridge, is a rare new-build hotel in the city. Its 85 accommodations, each designed by a team led by Antonio Citterio and Patricia Viel, feature lashings of leather, mahogany and stained oak, and all things luxe, as in the Bulgari III Suite (above). Six of the hotel's 12 floors are below ground, and its 47-seat cinema has a library of films curated by British director and producer David Puttnam. Il Ristorante, the in-house restaurant, is helmed by Robbie Pepin, who trained with Alain Ducasse. The jewel in Bulgari's new crown, though, is the two-floor spa (T 7151 1055), enhanced by a 25m pool (opposite) lined with green and gold mosaic tiles. *171 Knightsbridge, SW7, T 7151 1010, www.bulgarihotels.com/en-us/london*

St John Hotel

Fergus Henderson's nose-to-tail cooking manifesto has made him one of Britain's most influential chefs, and his St John restaurant (see p054) has long been the cornerstone of the Clerkenwell dining scene. In 2011, Henderson and business partner Trevor Gulliver took over the building once home to Manzi's seafood restaurant, a Soho institution well past its glory days, to open the St John Hotel. The 15 rooms are unfussy and compact, but extremely comfortable – with some designed simply for overnight stays after overindulging. You can also rent the entire top floor, including The Long Room (left), which makes a pleasant three-bedroom apartment. The restaurant is open from 8am for breakfast through to lunch, afternoon tea, supper and, if you're still hungry, late-night snacks. *1 Leicester Street, WC2, T 3301 8020, www.stjohnhotellondon.com*

40 Winks

When recommending a two-room hotel (with a shared bathroom, on the Mile End Road), there has to be something going on. And, at 40 Winks, there most definitely is. The four-floor Queen Anne townhouse is owned by stylist David Carter, whose design approach, although less restrained than our usual taste, does display a deft touch with overstuffed set pieces. The hotel is aimed squarely at media and creative types who are more concerned with visual stimulation than around-the-clock service. It has also built a reputation as a venue for chichi happenings, such as the Bedtime Story evenings, when, for a charge, actors and musicians perform short tales for pyjama-clad guests as they lounge in the drawing room (above).
109 Mile End Road, E1, T 7790 0259, www.40winks.org

Claridge's

Although it may be the de facto HQ of the European aristocracy, not even a hotel of Claridge's standing can afford to rest on its laurels. All of London's great hotels have had to update to survive and none has done so as successfully as this. In 2010, Diane von Furstenberg redesigned a series of rooms and suites, all of which feature her trademark prints and big, bold colours. DVF's two-bedroom Grand Piano Suite (above), which comes with butler service, is our favourite. Likewise, the hotel's public spaces, Gordon Ramsay's eponymous restaurant (T 7499 0099) among them, have also been restored to breathtaking effect by New York architect Thierry Despont. And – a detail that we love – the lift has its own driver and sofa. *Brook Street, W1, T 7629 8860, www.claridges.co.uk*

Café Royal
Opened in 1865, Café Royal was once
the haunt of bohemian London; Oscar
Wilde and Virginia Woolf were regulars.
Alfred and Georgi Akirov recruited
David Chipperfield to breathe new life
into the original features and create 159
rooms (Portland Junior Suite, pictured).
Six suites were sympathetically restored
by Donald Insall Associates.
68 Regent Street, W1, T 7406 3333

ME

At the western tip of the 1920s Aldwych crescent, next to Bush House (former home of the BBC World Service), this 157-room hotel is the work of Foster + Partners, from the outer shell to the bathroom fittings. The triangular building boasts a glass and Portland-stone facade, and oriel windows with views of the Strand and Somerset House. Its centrepiece, a 10-storey atrium housing a white marble lobby, is hidden at the core of the structure. The minimalist rooms, such as Aura (above), come with white leather walls and black lacquered cabinets; the penthouse Suite ME is topped by a glass cupola offering a panoramic vista. More landmark spotting, from Big Ben to Canary Wharf, can be done at the glam rooftop bar, Radio (T 7395 3440). *336-337 Strand, WC1, T 0845 601 8980, www.melondonuk.com*

Dorset Square Hotel

Marylebone is emerging as a hospitality hotspot. And any hospitality hotspot in London has to include a Firmdale hotel. Tim and Kit Kemp's group has seven in the city, and Dorset Square is the Firmdale modus operandi writ small. It has only 38 rooms spread over a townhouse that stands on the site of the first Lord's cricket ground. If the hotel is small and perfectly formed, its rooms, such as the Deluxe Garden View (above), still feature heaps of Kit Kemp's contemporary country-house furnishings, including fabrics produced with Christopher Farr, and objets trouvés collected on her global travels. There is an emphasis on cosy discretion at the Potting Shed bar and restaurant, and also in the domestic-scale drawing room.

39-40 Dorset Square, NW1, T 7723 7874, www.firmdalehotels.com

Boundary
Opened in 2009, this hotel tickles all of our fancies. It's small, with only 12 rooms and five suites; there's a great subterranean restaurant; a rooftop garden and grill; and a café/deli combo, Albion (T 7729 1051). It also has good green credentials. Each room has a designer or design movement as a theme so, among others, there's a Bauhaus Room (pictured) and an Eileen Gray Room. *2-4 Boundary Street, E2, T 7729 1051*

24 HOURS
SEE THE BEST OF THE CITY IN JUST ONE DAY

Just a quarter of a century ago, the presentation of Carl Andre's *Equivalent VIII*, better known as 'The Bricks', at the Tate gallery, now better known as Tate Britain (Millbank, SW1, T 7887 8888), caused much gnashing of teeth in London. (The Bricks remains a byword for crowd-displeasing conceptualism.)

Since the opening of Tate Modern (see p010) in 2000, the city, and visitors to it, have embraced contemporary art, and the gallery has become emblematic of London's re-emergence as a global creative hub. Our day takes in key new art sites, including Tate Modern's Tanks (see p034), a subterranean space designed for large-scale installations and performance art. But before this, we start at 19 Greek Street (opposite). From Bankside, we stroll to the south London outpost of White Cube (see p036). As is the way today, Jay Jopling's space is a commercial operation posing as an innovative public resource, and doing a good job of it.

We loop back to Soho's borders, to take in The Photographers' Gallery (see p037), before a ride to Shrimpy's (see p038), the long-term pop-up restaurant from art-world darlings David Waddington and Pablo Flack. Designed by architects Carmody Groarke, The Filling Station by night is a little bit of Ed Ruscha's LA on the edge of a London canal, standing alone and waiting for the biggest urban development in Europe to swallow it up.

For full addresses, see Resources.

10.00 19 Greek Street

The brainchild of Marc Péridis of interior design agency Montage, 19 Greek Street is six floors of design set in a handsome Victorian townhouse. The first and second levels of the gallery-cum-store are devoted to Espasso, the pioneering US showroom specialising in Brazilian design from the likes of Carlos Motta ('Asturias Armchair', above right). The remainder are peppered with products that prove sustainable design doesn't have to mean a sacrifice of style. There are pieces by Nina Tolstrup ('Pallet Chair', above left), Markus Kayser and Studio Aisslinger. The gallery will also be producing its own furniture – look out for exclusive collaborations, like Tolstrup and fashion designer David David's chair (above rear). Visits are by appointment.
19 Greek Street, W1, T 7734 5594,
www.19greekstreet.com

12.00 The Tanks
An exercise in less is more, Herzog & de Meuron's underground cylinders have alerted visitors to what Tate Modern is becoming: a unique contemporary art complex that can accommodate and inspire both the crowd-pleasing and the challenging. Sung Hwan Kim's *Temper Clay* (pictured) was one of the works commissioned for the launch.
Tate Modern, Bankside, SE1, T 7887 8888

WHITE CUBE

14.00 White Cube

Opened in 1993, Jay Jopling's first White Cube gallery was 4 sq m. His third, opened in 2011, is somewhat larger, at 5,400 sq m. It's a measure, literally, of how far Jopling's operation has come, but also of the degree to which the big-league art dealer has to come off as someone public-spirited these days. The most recent branch, a marker of Bermondsey's rebranding, has the size and the ambition of a public gallery, with 'museum-quality' exhibitions, a bookshop and an auditorium. Three large spaces show the artists White Cube represents, and three smaller areas provide a platform for younger talent. The gallery is housed in a 1970s warehouse, converted by Casper Mueller Kneer, whose smart adaptation of the canopy is another nod to Ed Ruscha. *144-152 Bermondsey Street, SE1, T 7930 5373, www.whitecube.com*

16.30 The Photographers' Gallery
In 1971, in a former Lyons tea bar in
Soho, Sue Davis launched the world's
first independent gallery devoted to
photography. Among those given their
first British shows there were Juergen
Teller, Andreas Gursky and Taryn Simon.
Outgrowing the site, The Photographers'
Gallery took a space on Ramillies Street in
2008 and, in 2010, embarked on a redesign
by Irish architects O'Donnell + Toumey.

Reopened in 2012, it now contains three
floors of exhibition space, including
a 'digital wall' (above, showing work by
Susan Sloan), a café, a bookshop and
print sales room. Intriguingly, the gallery
is pushing for the street outside to be
pedestrianised and to use the walls of
other buildings as further display space.
16-18 Ramillies Street, W1, T 7087 9300,
www.thephotographersgallery.org.uk

19.30 Shrimpy's

This venture by Bistrotheque's Pablo Flack and David Waddington is pulling London's young and fashionable to the new quarter taking shape in King's Cross. A Latin-American seafood restaurant, Shrimpy's moved into a former petrol filling station, given a new glow by Carmody Groarke's cinematic roof signage and illuminated fibreglass walls. The kiosk has become an intimate upmarket diner with wall doodles by Donald Urquhart, and the menu, by chef-director Tom Collins, is an epicurean's pan-American dream. Given the owners' standing with London's arts, fashion and media (and occasionally cross-dressing) crowds, it is a very social space. Opened in summer 2012 with an expected two-year lifespan, it already has a permanent feel. *The Filling Station, Goods Way, N1, T 8880 6111, www.shrimpys.co.uk*

URBAN LIFE

CAFÉS, RESTAURANTS, BARS AND NIGHTCLUBS

London has a nightlife proposition to rival any city. Its dining scene matches New York's for vibrancy and it boasts world-class restaurants. In fact, some of NYC's culinary movers and shakers have recently crossed the Atlantic to launch here. Daniel Boulud opened Bar Boulud (66 Knightsbridge, SW1, T 7201 3899) in the swank South-West, and Brit April Bloomfield, who charmed Gothamites with The Spotted Pig and The Breslin, is rumoured to be looking for a spot to create a new restaurant. Establishments such as Zucca (184 Bermondsey Street, SE1, T 7378 6809) and Hedone (301-303 Chiswick High Road, W4, T 8747 0377) prove that neighbourhood dining in the capital has risen to new level of sophistication. Mark Hix's room HIX (66-70 Brewer Street, W1, T 7292 3518) is where to sample cooking by the man who talked 'local' and 'seasonal' before they became tired tropes, while Oliver Dabbous is the new kid displaying a flair that has made his Fitzrovia venue Dabbous (see p055) the hottest table in town.

The rise of the small plate continues – butchery champions Brawn (49 Columbia Road, E2, T 7729 5692) and Polpo (see p047) still rank highly. London's bar life throws up the possibility of any kind of night out, from glam to grunge. Shoreditch House (Ebor Street, E1, T 7739 5040) looms large out east and Soho has been 'enlivened' by The Box (11-12 Walker's Court, W1, T 7434 4374). *For full addresses, see Resources.*

Pizarro

As the ex-executive chef at Brindisa in Borough Market, José Pizarro can make a legitimate claim to be the man who made Londoners tapas obsessives. We're not talking small plates or other tapas-alike innovations; and certainly not foam, mousse or other fluffed-up extractions. When Pizarro decided to go it alone, he moved only slightly east to Bermondsey Street, to open José (T 7403 4902), an authentic tapas bar with tiles, barrels, fantastic wines and sherries, *croquetas*, clams, chorizo and an unholy crush. He followed up with an eponymous restaurant, where you can sit down. There are still tiles, but also the same great cooking (Pizarro himself takes turns in the open kitchen), and the option of big-plate portions.
194 Bermondsey Street, SE1, T 7378 9455, www.josepizarro.com

Dock Kitchen

Now an elder statesman of British design, Tom Dixon is on a roll. Many fashionable bars and restaurants around the world seem to be illuminated by his designs, but he has also, almost by accident, turned into a successful restaurateur. Having launched as a pop-up at Dixon's Portobello Dock headquarters during the 2009 London Design Festival, the Dock Kitchen remains open and is one of London's more interesting dining rooms. The chef, Stevie Parle, formerly of the River Café, is an ex-supper-clubber who has built up a steady fan club. Although Parle has a particular fondness for subcontinental cooking, any trip here encourages country hopping from course to course. The room is like an extension of Dixon's studio – a showroom with table service – but, given his design nous, this is no bad thing. *344/342 Ladbroke Grove, W10, T 8962 1610, www.dockkitchen.co.uk*

Pollen Street Social
This Mayfair venue announces itself,
in a discreetly cheerful sort of way, as
something other than the traditional
fine-dining hall. What ex-Maze man
Jason Atherton is proposing is a foodie
hangout, with separate spaces for tapas
and cocktails, and a dessert bar. The
main action, though, is in Neri & Hu's
marvellous open-plan dining room.
8-10 Pollen Street, W1, T 7290 7600

Pizza East

Nick Jones, the man behind the Soho House group, is not infallible. The lifts at Shoreditch House are small and break down and, quite frankly, the members' list should be rethought. But when he gets things right, which is most of the time, he gets them very right. Jones' Pizza East, based, he says, on LA's Pizzeria Mozza and housed in Shoreditch's Tea Building (with Shoreditch House perched on top), is one of a new wave of high-quality pizza joints in the capital. Try the veal meatball pizza, and peruse the fantastic antipasti. The interior features exposed piping and concrete, stretches of leather, and a deli. There are now branches in Ladbroke Grove (T 8969 4500) and Kentish Town (T 3310 2000), neither technically 'East'.
56 Shoreditch High Street, E1,
T 7729 1888, www.pizzaeast.com

Polpo

This is the kind of bar/restaurant they do so effortlessly in Brooklyn or on the Lower East Side (bare bricks, tin ceiling, smallish square tables and no dinner reservations), but it always feels laboured when done in London. However, Polpo has pulled the trick off so well that it's become one of the most fashionable joints in town. The concept is a relocated *bacaro*: a type of Venetian bar dealing in Italianate tapas installed in an 18th-century Soho house that was once home to Canaletto. Such has been its success that versions have opened in Clerkenwell (T 7250 0034) and Covent Garden (T 7836 8448). Athough every second restaurant seems to serve tapas now, to our mind Polpo is up there with Morito (see p057) in terms of quality. *41 Beak Street, W1, T 7734 4479, www.polpo.co.uk*

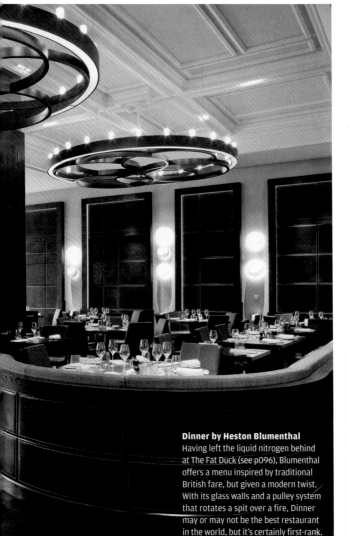

Dinner by Heston Blumenthal
Having left the liquid nitrogen behind
at The Fat Duck (see p096), Blumenthal
offers a menu inspired by traditional
British fare, but given a modern twist.
With its glass walls and a pulley system
that rotates a spit over a fire, Dinner
may or may not be the best restaurant
in the world, but it's certainly first-rank.
*Mandarin Oriental Hyde Park, 66
Knightsbridge, SW1, T 7201 3833*

Scott's

This restaurant has had the likes of Oscar Wilde and Ian Fleming through its doors over the past 150 years. By the end of the 20th century, though, Scott's had become the preserve of ageing pinstripes. It was acquired by Caprice Holdings in 2005 and designer Martin Brudnizki was called in to bring back the glam – and it has worked a treat. Scott's is updated deco done with real panache, and marked as utterly contemporary with artworks by Gary Hume and Fiona Rae, among others, and a giant crustacean shelf from Future Systems. There are oak and marble mosaic floors, and an onyx-topped, stingray-skinned oyster bar. Head chef Dave McCarthy produces some of the best seafood in town, completing the dining experience. *20 Mount Street, W1, T 7495 7309, www.scotts-restaurant.com*

Experimental Cocktail Club

A rare cross-channel transfer, ECC arrives courtesy of Romée de Goriainoff, Olivier Bon and Pierre-Charles Cros, who opened the first outpost in Paris in 2007, before bringing the concept to Chinatown. The interior, by Parisian designer Dorothée Meilichzon, is in a neo-speakeasy style, all the rage in New York but slow to take in London. There are plump love seats, a tin ceiling and a wooden bar with built-in piano. Staff wear sleeve garters and, if asked, will serve vintage spirits in vintage glasses. Despite being laid out over two floors, the place can cater for no more than 100 cocktail hounds, so conviviality is guaranteed. Settle in and try a Havana: an Old Fashioned made using a cigar-infused bourbon.
13a Gerrard Street, W1, T 7434 3559,
www.experimentalcocktailclublondon.com

Tramshed

Mark Hix, ex-head chef of Caprice Holdings, is one of the darlings of the London dining scene. With Tramshed, he goes back to Shoreditch. And back to basics. The restaurant serves chicken and steak, and little else. Hix was an early collector of Young British Artists, and Damien Hirst produced *Cock and Bull* – a pickled Hereford cow with a cockerel on its back – specifically for his new space. Hix has made an impressive dining hall of a listed power station, built in 1905 to provide the charge for the area's (long-gone) trams. It also houses Mark's Library Kitchen, where he holds cooking demonstrations. If you order the chicken, be warned that it arrives claws and all, skewered and upside down, to collect the juices. This isn't fine dining, but meaty, greasy-chinned indulgence.

32 Rivington Street, EC2, T 7749 0478, www.chickenandsteak.co.uk

St John Bread and Wine

Fergus Henderson, a trained architect, cooks with a modernist clarity of purpose. His Clerkenwell restaurant, St John (T 7251 0848), opened in 1994, certainly has a white-walled, spare seriousness about it, while his modern British menu, which has a famed emphasis on offal, is puritan in its lack of elaboration. Having firmly established St John among the Clerkenwell creative set, Henderson branched out in 2003 with St John Bread and Wine in Spitalfields. As the name quietly suggests, this space is part bakery, part wine shop, as well as an all-day restaurant, but with a far simpler menu than the mothership. Breakfast is especially good; it would be wise to order the smoked Gloucester Old Spot bacon sandwich.
94-96 Commercial Street, E1, T 3301 8069, www.stjohnbreadandwine.com

Dabbous

The power of Fay Maschler – the Pauline Kael of British food critics – and a Twitter frenzy have made getting a reservation at London's table of the moment an exercise in delayed gratification (eager diners face a 10-month wait). It doesn't hurt that chef Oliver Dabbous looks like a rock star. But it's his cooking that is raising temperatures. Dabbous worked with Raymond Blanc at Le Manoir aux Quat'Saisons and at Texture in London, topping up his training with stints at the Fat Duck, Noma and Hibiscus. The menu is short and the food is simple, in that intense-flavoured way. Brinkworth's interior is classic bare-duct functionalism, but with great attention to detail. If you can't wait, a better class of snacks and cocktails are served in the basement bar, helmed by co-owner Oskar Kinberg. *39 Whitfield Street, W1, T 7323 1544*

Brasserie Zédel

When Oliver Peyton opened the Atlantic Bar & Grill in the old Regent Palace Hotel in 1994, it created a new calculus of cool in the capital. The Atlantic was enormous *and* fashionable. Eventually, though, the numbers stopped adding up and it closed in 2005. Now the space has been reworked as a Paris-style restaurant called Brasserie Zédel. The scale of the place still impresses, and it has been kitted out in belle époque finery by David Collins. You still enter down a grand staircase into a foyer. The titanic dining room is ahead; other doors lead to Bar Americain and the Crazy Coqs cabaret bar. A venture of Chris Corbin and Jeremy King, Zédel takes the fin de siècle shtick that worked so well at The Wolseley and The Delaunay, and drops the prices, on a menu that is a Francophile fantasy.
20 Sherwood Street, W1, T 7734 4888

Morito

For more than a decade, Samuel and Samantha Clark's Moro (T 7833 8336) has exerted a quiet but powerful pull on the city's diners. In 2010, they took over the space next door, previously occupied by Brindisa – London's leading *nuevo tapas* exponents – for their take on an Iberian bar-with-nibbles. The tapas are deliciously innovative, without moving away from core principles, although there are some Middle Eastern and North African touches. Standouts include the pork belly with cumin and lemon. The wine list is worth investigating, and small dishes are usually served without having to book, so a wait to join the scrum at the packed bar is to be expected and should be enjoyed as part of the Morito experience.
32 Exmouth Market, EC1, T 7278 7007, www.morito.co.uk

NOPI
Yotam Ottolenghi, the Israeli-born chef behind an empire of deli/cafés, has finally opened his first restaurant, a ground-floor dining room dressed in cleanly cut marble and brass, and a basement brasserie. Superior Middle Eastern cuisine is served from breakfast to dinner. NOPI also boasts some of the glammest bathrooms in London.
21-22 Warwick Street, W1, T 7494 9584

L'Anima

Architect Claudio Silvestrin pulled off an expensive minimalist aesthetic at L'Anima, engineering a space of cool drama with travertine floors and marble bathrooms. A glass wall separates the dining room from the bar (above), where the porphyry walls are the perfect complement to the white leather seats. A curving corridor leads to a walk-in wine cellar and a private dining room with a green marble table.

The restaurant's founder is Italian chef Francesco Mazzei, formerly of St Alban. At L'Anima, he and his talented team cook impeccable, mostly southern Italian food. Try the linguine with hand-picked crab, chilli and Amalfi lemon, or the fettuccine with wild mushrooms, followed by Calabrian dark-chocolate iced truffle. *1 Snowden Street, EC2, T 7422 7000, www.lanima.co.uk*

The Connaught Bar

Built in 1897, The Connaught is the very definition of the London luxury hotel as urban country house. It has promised and delivered discretion and a fierce resistance to novelty. By 2004, though, when it was bought by the Maybourne Hotel Group (owners of Claridge's and the Berkeley), The Connaught was considered a little too Wodehousian to be entirely healthy. The ensuing £70m overhaul included the complete reimagining of its two bars. India Mahdavi redesigned the Coburg Bar (T 7499 7070), and heavyweight champ of bar designers David Collins added oodles of glamour to the Connaught Bar (above), which has its own entrance on Mount Street. The interior cocoons you amid marble and black leather banquettes. *Carlos Place, W1, T 7314 3419, www.the-connaught.co.uk*

INSIDER'S GUIDE

KIRSTY CARTER, GRAPHIC DESIGNER

Kirsty Carter is a director of design agency A Practice for Everyday Life (www.apracticeforeverydaylife.com), whose clients include the Barbican (see p071) and Tate Britain (see p032). She lives in Victoria Park Village, which she describes as 'East London's little secret'. Her favourite shops here include Haus (39 Morpeth Road, E9, T 7536 9291), which sells household objects, and Bottle Apostle (95 Lauriston Road, E9, T 8985 1549), 'where I can pick up nice wine when I'm cooking dinner at home,' she says.

Carter often eats out at Nuno Mendes' Corner Room at the Town Hall Hotel (see p016); for lunch, she likes Rochelle Canteen (Rochelle School, Arnold Circus, E2, T 7729 5677). She's also a fan of Shrimpy's (see p038) in King's Cross: 'It's a piece of Mexico-slash-California in London.' For coffee, her pick is Climpson & Sons (67 Broadway Market, E8), and her late-night drinking venue of choice is neo-speakeasy Nightjar (129 City Road, EC1, T 7253 4101).

When shopping, Carter visits Lamb's Conduit Street. 'This is a lovely street to browse along and it has great clothes shops, like Folk (No 53, WC1, T 8616 4191) and Oliver Spencer (No 58, WC1, T 7831 3483).' Her bookshop tip is Artwords, which has branches on Broadway Market (T 7923 7507) and Rivington Street (T 7729 2000). Rough Trade East (Dray Walk, 91 Brick Lane, E1, T 7392 7788), is her one stop for 'impromptu gigs and the best records'. *For full addresses, see Resources.*

ARCHITOUR

A GUIDE TO LONDON'S ICONIC BUILDINGS

When Ernö Goldfinger's 1960s cinema at Elephant and Castle was torn down in 1988, it was little lamented. In those days, London seemed to be determined only to replace its modernist heritage with anodyne office blocks, peddling nothing more interesting than 1980s aspiration. That the city largely failed in that mission is one of Europe's better-kept architectural secrets. London's modernist legacy is one of its least-appreciated treats.

Nowhere, save the better stations on the Jubilee Line, can remove you so totally from the blitzed and otherwise edited mess of histories that make up the city as the Barbican development does (see p071). Walk along its elevated walkways and lakes set in concrete and you're in a cohesive retro futurescape, a fragment of a different city. Although the first plans were drawn up by Chamberlin, Powell & Bon in 1955, their work was not completed until the opening of the Barbican arts complex in 1982. By then, it looked out of date. Today, it looks like a dream.

The development of the King's Cross area dwarfs even the ambition of the Barbican scheme. John McAslan's new concourse at King's Cross station (see p068) is the clearest demonstration yet of how bold and beautiful this district of the city could be. Meanwhile, in the City, New Court (see p066) is a graceful tower that makes much around it look lumpen and ill-conceived. *For full addresses, see Resources.*

Economist Building

Peter and Alison Smithson were (almost) the Charles and Ray Eames of postwar Britain, being among the country's most important modernists and creators of the 'new brutalist' movement. In truth, they talked and theorised more than they built, but the Economist Building, commissioned in 1960 and completed in 1964, is their masterpiece. Actually comprising three Portland-stone towers set around a plaza in the mostly Palladian St James's, the complex had to include not only the offices of *The Economist* – as well as a penthouse for the newspaper's chairman Geoffrey Crowther – but a bank, shops and serviced flats for the Boodle's club next door. Their clients insisted that they build a hymn to modernity, with 'no fake antiquarianism'. And that is certainly what they delivered.
25 St James's Street, SW1

New Court

OMA's new home for Rothschild (the practice's first London building) is the most exciting addition to the 'Cityscape' in years. A 10-storey mesh cube, topped by a two-floor 'sky pavilion', it displays a lightness of touch that is missing from Norman Foster's Walbrook Building, the still-unoccupied metal blob that it overlooks. Nathan Mayer Rothschild first moved to the St Swithin's Lane site in 1809. This fourth headquarters of the family business, now a financial advisory company, opened its doors at the end of 2011. Given that the lane is a skinny medieval cut-through, it's hard to take in the facade at street level. What you do get is a marble forecourt and, for the first time in 200 years, views through to Christopher Wren's St Stephen Walbrook church.

New Court, St Swithin's Lane, EC4

The Shard

It can seem at times as if the London skyline is being devised by a seven-year-old boy, with its wheels, pyramids and rockets. Rising 310m above the low-rise Victorian red brick of Borough High Street, Renzo Piano's glazed spire is an astonishing sight. It has 72 storeys, 44 lifts and will house penthouses, offices, restaurants and a Shangri-La hotel. It is not, of course, without its critics. It interrupts many of the city's supposedly protected views; it is, in essence, a giant glass tower when giant glass towers have a bad rap (20 per cent of the steelwork used, though, was recycled, as were 95 per cent of the other materials). Dubai-style horror or not, the structure has an elegance and ambition that most locals admire.
32 London Bridge Street, SE1,
www.the-shard.com

King's Cross Western Concourse

Thanks to the relocations of *The Guardian* newspaper and Central Saint Martins art college, the area north of King's Cross station is starting to feel like the buzzing new quarter that has long been promised (even if a lot of the area's 27 hectares of brownfield land still look brown and field-like). And the terminus itself finally looks like the anchor tenant of a lively new 'hood. From the outside, John McAslan's Western Concourse resembles a giant flying saucer that has crashed into the Victorian hulk of the 1852 station. Inside, it is a vast open dome, ascending 20m into the air, with a span of 52m. The dome grows out of a 16-part steel stalk, which opens out into a dazzling latticework of branches that plant themselves back into a public plaza. There are 28 shops in the new concourse, but it feels less like an upmarket mall than neighbouring St Pancras.
Euston Road/York Way, N1

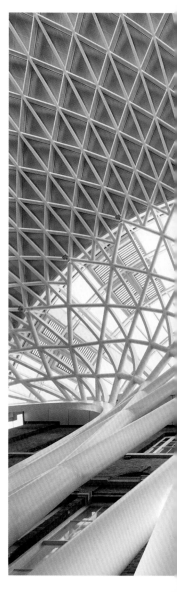

National Theatre

This is the most visible example of heroic modernism in London. Denys Lasdun's design had to include three theatres and all sorts of backstage spaces, as well as cafés, bars and foyers, yet the building remains one of the most dramatic to grace the River Thames. The interiors are just as impressive; the largest being the Olivier Theatre (named after the National's founder). A two-phase renovation will see the smallest theatre, the Cottesloe, close in late 2013 (reopening as the Dorfman Theatre in 2014), with work due to continue into 2015. Although the scheme will include the creation of additional public space, the site should remain a perfect expression of Lasdun's ambition, as if he sought to make landscapes of buildings. *South Bank, SE1, T 7452 3400, www.nationaltheatre.org.uk*

Barbican

Architects Chamberlin, Powell & Bon had complete control of the Barbican development, right down to the doorknobs. Eventually, it would include three towers of more than 40 storeys each, 13 terrace blocks, one seven-storey tower, a church, two schools and the Barbican Centre arts complex (in truth, something of an afterthought). The architects referenced Frank Lloyd Wright and Le Corbusier, but came up with something unique, working on it from 1955 until 1982. In 2001, the concert hall was improved by Kirkegaard Associates and Caruso St John, and Allford Hall Monaghan Morris reworked the Art Gallery in 2004. Fortuitously, where the Barbican was once a little lost in a forgotten part of town, it is now in the heart of the fashionable 'east side'. *EC2, T 7638 4141, www.barbican.org.uk*

SHOPPING

THE BEST RETAIL THERAPY AND WHAT TO BUY

This is a city with two of the most innovative department stores in the world: Selfridges (400 Oxford Street, W1, T 0800 123 400) and Liberty (see p081). Nearby Bond Street may be predictable, but it's bountiful, and Mayfair also has the exciting Dover Street Market (see p084). There's far more to London's retail scene than that, however, from the swish outlets that line Marylebone High Street to the low-key boutiques of Lamb's Conduit Street, such as Darkroom (see p082), and the offerings of Shoreditch, including menswear store Present (140 Shoreditch High Street, E1, T 7033 0500), which boasts a barista. Round the corner, Jasper Morrison celebrates 'Super Normal' design at his store (see p076), and Redchurch Street is gathering pace as a shopping hotspot. North of here, in Dalston, LN-CC (see p074) is reinventing the concept store as conceptual store, with an appointment-only retail theatre backed by an online shop to handle most of the transactions.

London has become an art-world hub, with Mayfair galleries such as White Cube (25-26 Mason's Yard, SW1, T 7930 5373), which now has a branch in Bermondsey (see p036), Haunch of Venison (103 New Bond Street, W1, T 7495 5050) and Hauser & Wirth (23 Savile Row, W1, T 7287 2300) leading the pack. Design galleries are moving in too. Pay a visit to Carpenters Workshop Gallery (3 Albemarle Street, W1, T 3051 5939) and 19 Greek Street (see p033). *For full addresses, see Resources.*

David Gill Galleries

This is one of our favourite resources. David Gill's vast gallery in a disused glove-and-handbag factory in south London is where to go for one-off, modern, sculptural pieces and works by Barnaby Barford, Fredrikson Stallard, Mattia Bonetti and Zaha Hadid, among others. Items are sold in editions of six to 30 and are the museum collectables of the future. From his Loughborough Street location, Gill sells modern classics by designers including Charlotte Perriand and Jean Prouvé, such as the 1952 'Tunisie' bookshelf (above), price on request. Gill launched his first store in 1987 and he's been driving the market for 20th- and 21st-century design ever since. His latest venture on King Street (T 3195 6600) carries on that tradition. *3 Loughborough Street, SE11, T 7793 1100, www.davidgillgalleries.com*

Late Night Chameleon Cafe
This new-model 'curated' concept store sells hard-to-find designers (many of them exclusive to LN-CC outside Asia), top-notch audio equipment and rare books. The distinctive interior was conceived by set-designer Gary Card and, despite being appointment only, the shop is no too-cool snootsphere. Once you're in, the welcome is warm.
18 Shacklewell Lane, E8, T 7275 7265

Jasper Morrison Shop

The British designer Jasper Morrison is enjoying a moment, a serious moment. After a period of time in which certain elements of the design world became overelaborate and overexcited at being told they were artists, and were paid accordingly, Morrison held steady with his quietly militant dedication to 'everyday useful objects', the 'Super Normal', as he called it. Together with Japanese designer Naoto Fukasawa, Morrison put together an exhibition of the Super Normal, and this shop, a small, unused area of his studio in Shoreditch, continues that project, stocking his own designs, those by other members of the Super Normal crew, and further anonymous examples of the elegantly practical. Closed at weekends. *24b Kingsland Road, E2, www.jaspermorrison.com/shop*

Labour and Wait

A celebration of functional design from an age before anyone thought to fetishise functionalism, Labour and Wait was established in 2000 by designers Rachel Wythe-Moran and Simon Watkins. The duo were frustrated that the fast pace of fashion did not allow for the maturing of items into classics. In 2010, the brand moved from a rather artfully crammed store on Cheshire Street to a slightly larger space on Redchurch Street. Here, you can pick up hardware for the kitchen and garden, as well as utilitarian clothing, stationery and accessories. Standout items include the extensive selection of enamel tableware and utensils, ranging from delicate milk pans to not-so-delicate pie dishes. Closed on Mondays.
85 Redchurch Street, E2, T 7729 6253, www.labourandwait.co.uk

Charlotte Olympia

A graduate of London's Cordwainers school, Charlotte Dellal launched her first shoe collection in 2008. The daughter of ex-model Andrea and sister of socialite Alice, her shoes are heavy on 1940s glamour with just the right amount of wit; Dellal also dresses like she could whistle up with Humphrey Bogart. In 2010, she opened a store, Charlotte Olympia, in Mayfair. The space makes a star of the shoes and, with names like Dolly, Maxine and Ursula, sees them elevated on brass stands or encased in glass cabinets. Guarded by an ornamental leopard in the window, the shop is otherwise stylishly restrained and has parquet floors and midcentury furniture. Browse the clutches and hosiery, also designed by Dellal.
56 Maddox Street, W1, T 7499 0145, www.charlotteolympia.com

Hostem

Shoreditch may have been forsaken by the hipsters, who have headed north and east for their late-night clubbing thrills, but, by day, its retail scene gets more interesting. This menswear store presents a smart array of international labels, from Adam Kimmel to Visvim, and has a startlingly spare interior by rising design duo James Russell and Hannah Plumb, collectively JamesPlumb. Here, they've created hybrid designs by reusing old pieces of furniture and materials, infusing them with wit and charm. The space is split into three areas. There's one room for streetwear, one for avant-garde fashion and a third for 'visiting' designers. As a whole, the shop seems to summon the Victorian spirits said to haunt the area.
41-43 Redchurch Street, E2, T 7739 9733, www.hostem.co.uk

Liberty

Renowned for its trademark prints, this London bastion has long been synonymous with luxury and international design. The Regent Street shop, stocked with decorative homewares and objets d'art from North Africa, Japan and the East, was opened in 1875 by Arthur Liberty, who did not want 'to follow existing fashions, but to create new ones'. The Tudor-style building, designed by Edwin T Hall and his son Edwin S Hall, was constructed in 1924 from the timbers of two ships. More recently, it has become a cutting-edge emporium following a strategic tune-up. The imaginative, focused buying skills of the fashion department are more akin to a sharp-minded independent than a generic, label-bagging department store. *210-220 Regent Street, W1, T 7734 1234, www.liberty.co.uk*

Darkroom

Thanks to a highly principled landlord, Holborn's Lamb's Conduit Street is a shining example of fine retailing. Compact concept store Darkroom arrived in 2009. Mixing interior accessories and original high-end fashion, founders and friends Rhonda Drakeford and Lulu Roper-Caldbeck go global to source beautiful pieces that are unique to the store. The pair are also peddling their own, highly covetable designs, as well as hosting bimonthly art and sculpture exhibitions. Darkroom is worth visiting, if for no other reason than to check out the shop's immaculate styling. Design team Matt Edmonds and Pam West, of Frank, have created bespoke shelving, a cash desk and display cabinets for the shop, whereas the statement tiled floor was hand-painted by the talented proprietors themselves.
52 Lamb's Conduit Street, WC1, T 7831 7244, www.darkroomlondon.com

Dover Street Market

Mindful that the super-architect-designed 'luxury box' was becoming a cliché, Comme des Garçons' Rei Kawakubo founded DSM in a Georgian townhouse-turned-office in 2004, spending a piffling £800,000 on the refurb, gutting the place and giving it a cursory paint job. Interior design, such as it is, was left to film and set designers. Essentially, Kawakubo's guerrilla store concept is a collection of 'shabbily' artful stalls put together by her own various Comme incarnations, major names such as Ann Demeulemeester, Givenchy and Lanvin, and some more esoteric set-ups, including retro-hardware store Labour and Wait (see p077). Dover Street Market can also be credited with leading the retail migration west of Bond Street. *17-18 Dover Street, W1, T 7518 0680, www.doverstreetmarket.com*

Mint

Established by Lina Kanafani in the late 1990s, Mint is the kind of design store that goes far beyond the usual suspects, commissioning exclusive one-off and limited-edition products from new and established designers, in addition to handcrafted glass, ceramics and textiles. The joy of Mint is Kanafani's fearlessness and aversion to the safety of quiet good taste. Mint challenges you to get to grips with Kanafani's selection, to take your time, and to come back once you have thought it over. It's a strategy that has paid off handsomely. Since 2009, regular Minters have had to get used to going back to the newer, larger store in the Brompton Quarter (above) and not the tiny original shop on Wigmore Street. *2 North Terrace, SW3, T 7225 2228, www.mintshop.co.uk*

Margaret Howell
A long-serving stalwart of British
fashion, Margaret Howell has enjoyed
a major renaissance as a champion of
clean, immaculately tailored British
casualwear for men and women. Her
flagship store on Wigmore Street,
designed by William Russell of
Pentagram, also displays new and
vintage UK modernist furniture.
34 Wigmore Street, W1, T 7009 9009

SPORTS AND SPAS

WORK OUT, CHILL OUT OR JUST WATCH

The 2012 Olympics left London with some fine and architecturally daring sports arenas. Zaha Hadid's Aquatics Centre and Hopkins Architects' marvellous Velodrome (see p090), where Team GB showed the rest of the world a clean pair of heels, are the crown jewels of Queen Elizabeth Olympic Park in Newham, East London. Both these venues will eventually be open to the public, as will new outdoor road circuits and off-road trails at the VeloPark.

The city also boasts what Norman Foster calls the world's finest football ground: Wembley Stadium (Empire Way, HA9, T 0844 980 8001). One of London's iconic structures, it has a huge illuminated arch, and facilities that are a vast improvement on its predecessor.

In truth, squeezing sport and fitness into London life isn't easy. But there are excellent gyms – try The Third Space (13 Sherwood Street, W1, T 7439 6333) or Matt Roberts (16 Berkeley Street, W1, T 7491 9989) – good football pitches, decent climbing centres and great spas, such as the Dorchester Spa (Park Lane, W1, T 7319 7109) and the Cowshed treatment rooms at Shoreditch House (see p040). Among London's neglected treasures are its lidos, including the lovely London Fields Lido (London Fields West Side, E8, T 7254 9038), while the Thames is, of course, famous for its rowing clubs. Finally, the provision of cycle lanes is slowly getting better as the number of riders on the roads increases exponentially. *For full addresses, see Resources.*

Dunhill

In 2008, Dunhill opened a retail store-cum-exclusive members' hangout in an 18th-century grand pile – very grand, as it was once the home of the Duke of Westminster, on Davies Street, just north of Berkeley Square. Our favourite feature of the house is its wonderful spa and barber's (above), which is a witty and thoroughly welcoming update of the traditional gentlemen's grooming parlour – think Geo F Trumper et al. Customers even get their own TV screen, so they can watch a movie while enjoying tonsorial attention. In addition to the wet shaves and short-back-and-sides administered here, two treatment rooms host more modern forms of pampering, including hot-stone and sports massages, and facials. Closed on Sundays.
2 Davies Street, W1, T 7853 4440, www.dunhill.com

Velodrome

Post-Gherkin (see p012), any new London building without right angles in all the right places is liable to be saddled with an affectionate (often food-based) nickname. And so Hopkins Architects' Velodrome has been tagged the 'Pringle'. And indeed it does resemble a Pringle crisp, its angled wooden oval (a hyperbolic paraboloid if you prefer) directly referencing the track within. Fittingly, given Britain's recent emergence as a cycling superpower, it was the first of the Olympic Park stadia to be completed. And, along with Zaha Hadid's Aquatics Centre, it is an architectural high. (Make's handball arena, the Copper Box, is a small triumph too.) The Velodrome is also the most sustainable of the Park's venues, its red cedar bowl again referencing the sustainably sourced pine track.

Olympic Park, E20

Laban Building

Built in 2002 for £22m, the Laban Building at Trinity Laban Conservatoire of Music and Dance is one of the largest and most expensive contemporary dance centres in the world. It was designed by Herzog & de Meuron and is, many would say, their most important contribution to London's landscape (even if Laban's position on a former rubbish tip in Deptford means not enough people get to see it). Designed in collaboration with artist Michael Craig-Martin, the building is a polycarbonate-coated box that allows shadowy views of the student dancers during the day. At night, it becomes a giant lantern, lit up in lime, turquoise and magenta. The interior is no less successful, with a Pilates studio, health suite, 300-seat theatre and café. *Creekside, SE8, T 8691 8600, www.laban.org*

Lord's

It seems odd that the Marylebone Cricket Club, the ultra-conservative high court of English cricket, should commission such an outlandish structure. In fact, the lords of Lord's are daring patrons of innovative architecture. Witness Future Systems' Media Centre (above), finished in 1999, at roughly the same time as Nicholas Grimshaw's grandstand. The Media Centre still startles. Built using shipbuilding and aircraft technology, it was the world's first all-aluminium semi-monocoque building. And it's not often we get to say that. Its purpose is to contain all the TV, radio and press people under one roof. Raised 14m above the Compton and Edrich Stands, it looks like the sinister eye of a monstrous machine, which it kind of is. *St John's Wood Road, NW8, T 7616 8500, www.lords.org*

Aman Spa at The Connaught
Following a £70m makeover, completed
in 2009, The Connaught has shaken off
its reputation as a discreet but dusty old
dame. Among its highlights is the UK's
first Aman Spa, which offers treatments
from around the globe. Expect Aman's
trademark minimal orientalism, including
a small but tranquil pool (pictured).
Carlos Place, W1, T 3147 7305,
www.the-connaught.co.uk

ESCAPES

WHERE TO GO IF YOU WANT TO LEAVE TOWN

London has no Hamptons or Sitges, although the Cotswolds to the west and Norfolk to the north are strong weekend draws. Both now have good stocks of delis, design shops, excellent restaurants, old pubs gone gourmet and contemporary country-house hotels, including Cowley Manor (Cowley, Gloucestershire, T 01242 870 900) and Babington House (Babington, Somerset, T 01373 812 266). Closer to the capital, in Berkshire, Coworth Park (Blacknest Road, Ascot, T 01344 876 600), part of the Dorchester Collection, is traditional but plenty luxe, with a first-rate spa. The Olde Bell Inn (see p102) is less grand, but just as welcome an innovation.

The village of Bray in Berkshire has become a genuine global gastro-resort. Here, Heston Blumenthal cooks up snail porridge, quail jelly and the other classic dishes of his now-notorious 'molecular gastronomy' repertoire at the three-Michelin-starred Fat Duck (High Street, T 01628 580 333). Its near-neighbour, the similarly bestowed Waterside Inn (Ferry Road, T 01628 620 691), is now headed up by chef Alain Roux, son of Michel.

London's nearest major seaside resort is trendy Brighton, just 70km away. It is full of fine Regency architecture, including the bizarre Royal Pavilion (Old Steine, T 01273 290 900). There are also several handsome examples of modernism located close to London, such as The Homewood (see p100) in Surrey.
For full addresses, see Resources.

De La Warr Pavilion, Bexhill-on-Sea
Completed in 1935, Erich Mendelsohn and Serge Chermayeff's De La Warr Pavilion, situated on the East Sussex coast, was the country's first modernist public building. In 1933, the competition to construct a seaside entertainment complex was announced within a couple of months of Mendelsohn arriving in England, and the German émigré, already a renowned figure in European architecture, hit the project at some speed. He created an impossibly glamorous docked-liner of a structure, with large glass windows and curving terraces, and an enormous chrome-and-steel staircase. An £8m restoration project by architects John McAslan helped to re-establish the Pavilion as one of southern England's most important cultural buildings. *Marina, T 01424 229 111, www.dlwp.com*

Turner Contemporary, Margate

A faded seaside town in Kent, Margate is probably now best known for its part in Tracey Emin's open wound of a life story. 'Whatever I do, part of Margate always comes with me,' she said. It seems right, then, that an art gallery is being viewed as a lever for the town's reversal of terminal decline. The Turner Contemporary, which was designed by David Chipperfield and opened in 2011, is named after Margate's other artist-in-residence, JMW Turner, who went to school here and returned often, because he loved the light (and a local hotel keeper). Chipperfield's building, a series of elegant, angular art sheds, is built on the site of the guesthouse where Turner painted, and is mostly about the wonders it plays with light on the inside. *Rendezvous, T 01843 233 000, www.turnercontemporary.org*

The Homewood, Esher
A counterpoint to Surrey's wealthy but dull stockbroker belt, The Homewood is essentially an open-plan glass-and-air take on the country house. Completed in 1938 by Patrick Gwynne, a modernist who worked alongside Wells Coates and studied the work of Le Corbusier, the property makes use of marble, terrazzo and gold leaf to stunning effect.
Portsmouth Road, T 01372 476 424

The Olde Bell Inn, Hurley
In some ways, The Olde Bell Inn (10 minutes from Henley-on-Thames) simply reflects the boutique-ing and gastro-ising of the traditional British coaching inn. Rooms that were once fusty and stale-smelling now feature walk-in monsoon showers and Aesop toiletries. But designer Ilse Crawford has managed to assemble private and public spaces that sit easily with the history of this wonky Tudor building – some parts of which actually date as far back as 1135. In the dining room, banquettes are brightened with geometric-print Welsh blankets, and contemporary Thonet bentwood chairs are matched with Matthew Hilton for Ercol's birch Windsors, produced in High Wycombe. The food, by chef Damian Broom, which, of course, makes use of locally sourced ingredients, is terrific.
High Street, T 01628 825 881,
www.theoldebell.co.uk

NOTES
SKETCHES AND MEMOS

RESOURCES
CITY GUIDE DIRECTORY

A

Albion 030
Boundary
2-4 Boundary Street, E2
T 7729 1051
www.albioncaff.co.uk

Aman Spa at The Connaught 094
Carlos Place, W1
T 3147 7305
www.the-connaught.co.uk

L'Anima 060
1 Snowden Street, EC2
T 7422 7000
www.lanima.co.uk

Artwords 062
20-22 Broadway Market, E8
T 7923 7507
69 Rivington Street, EC2
T 7729 2000
www.artwords.co.uk

B

Bar Boulud 040
Mandarin Oriental Hyde Park
66 Knightsbridge, SW1
T 7201 3899
www.danielnyc.com

Barbican 071
EC2
T 7638 4141
www.barbican.org.uk

Bottle Apostle 062
95 Lauriston Road, E9
T 8985 1549
www.bottleapostle.com

The Box 040
11-12 Walker's Court, W1
T 7434 4374
www.theboxsoho.com

Brasserie Zédel 056
20 Sherwood Street, W1
T 7734 4888
www.brasseriezedel.com

Brawn 040
49 Columbia Road, E2
T 7729 5692
www.brawn.co

BT Tower 014
60 Cleveland Street, W1

Bulgari Spa 020
Bulgari
171 Knightsbridge, SW7
T 7151 1055
www.bulgarihotels.com/en-us/london

C

Carpenters Workshop Gallery 072
3 Albemarle Street, W1
T 3051 5939
www.cwgdesign.com

Centre Point 013
101-103 New Oxford Street, WC1

Charlotte Olympia 078
56 Maddox Street, W1
T 7499 0145
www.charlotteolympia.com

Climpson & Sons 062
67 Broadway Market, E8
www.webcoffeeshop.co.uk

Coburg Bar 061
The Connaught
Carlos Place, W1
T 7499 7070
www.the-connaught.co.uk

The Connaught Bar 061
The Connaught
Carlos Place, W1
T 7314 3419
www.the-connaught.co.uk

HOTELS
ADDRESSES AND ROOM RATES

Babington House 096
Room rates:
double, from £250
Babington
Somerset
T 01373 812 266
www.babingtonhouse.co.uk

Boundary 030
Room rates:
double, from £205;
Bauhaus Room, from £205;
Eileen Gray Room, from £230;
Suites, from £350
2-4 Boundary Street, E2
T 7729 1051
www.theboundary.co.uk

Bulgari 020
Room rates:
double, from £440;
Bulgari III Suite, £8,500
171 Knightsbridge, SW7
T 7151 1010
www.bulgarihotels.com/en-us/london

Café Royal 026
Room rates:
double, from £450;
Portland Junior Suite, £1,100
68 Regent Street, W1
T 7406 3333
www.hotelcaferoyal.com

Claridge's 025
Room rates:
double, from £360;
Grand Piano Suite, from £7,800
Brook Street, W1
T 7629 8860
www.claridges.co.uk

Corinthia 016
Room rates:
double, from £450
Whitehall Place, SW1
T 7930 8181
www.corinthia.com

Cowley Manor 096
Room rates:
double, from £295
Cowley
Gloucestershire
T 01242 870 900
www.cowleymanor.com

Coworth Park 096
Room rates:
double, from £235
Blacknest Road
Ascot
Berkshire
T 01344 876 600
www.coworthpark.com

The Dorchester 016
Room rates:
double, from £360
Park Lane, W1
T 7629 8888
www.thedorchester.com

Dorset Square Hotel 029
Room rates:
double, from £235;
Deluxe Garden View Room, £355
39-40 Dorset Square, NW1
T 7723 7874
www.firmdalehotels.com

40 Winks 024
Room rates:
double, from £185
109 Mile End Road, E1
T 7790 0259
www.40winks.org

ME 028
Room rates:
double, from £400;
Aura, from £400;
Suite ME, £7,200
336-337 Strand, WC1
T 0845 601 8980
www.melondonuk.com

The Olde Bell Inn 102
Room rates:
double from, £115
High Street
Hurley
Berkshire
T 01628 825 881
www.theoldebell.co.uk

The Savoy 017
Room rates:
double, from £350
Strand, WC2
T 7836 4343
www.fairmont.com/savoy

St John Hotel 022
Room rates:
double, from £180;
The Long Room, £320
1 Leicester Street, WC2
T 3301 8020
www.stjohnhotellondon.com

St Pancras Renaissance 018
Room rates:
double, from £265;
Chambers Junior Suite, from £505
Euston Road, NW1
T 7841 3540
www.marriott.co.uk

10 Trinity Square 016
Room rates:
prices on request
10 Trinity Square, EC3
www.10trinitysquare.com

Town Hall Hotel & Apartments 016
Room rates:
double, from £175
Patriot Square, E2
T 7871 0460
www.townhallhotel.com

The Zetter 016
Room rates:
double, from £220
St John's Square
86-88 Clerkenwell Road, EC1
T 7324 4444
www.thezetter.com

WALLPAPER* CITY GUIDES

Executive Editor
Rachael Moloney

Author
Nick Compton

Art Director
Loran Stosskopf
Art Editor
Eriko Shimazaki
Designer
Mayumi Hashimoto
Map Illustrator
Russell Bell

Photography Editor
Elisa Merlo
Photography Assistant
Nabil Butt

Chief Sub-Editor
Nick Mee
Sub-Editors
Emily Brooks
Julia Chadwick

Editorial Assistant
Emma Harrison

Interns
Laura Font Sentis
Aiko Koike

Wallpaper* Group
Editor-in-Chief
Tony Chambers
Publishing Director
Gord Ray
Managing Editor
Jessica Diamond
Acting Managing Editor
Oliver Adamson

First published 2006
Revised and updated
2007, 2009, 2010, 2011
and 2013

© 2006, 2007, 2009,
2010, 2011 and 2013
IPC Media Limited

ISBN 978 0 7148 6460 0

All prices are correct at
the time of going to press,
but are subject to change.

Printed in China

PHAIDON

Phaidon Press Limited
Regent's Wharf
All Saints Street
London N1 9PA

Phaidon Press Inc
180 Varick Street
New York, NY 10014

Phaidon® is a registered
trademark of Phaidon
Press Limited

www.phaidon.com

A CIP Catalogue record for
this book is available from
the British Library.

PHOTOGRAPHERS

Richard Bryant/Arcaid
Turner Contemporary,
pp098-099

Emma Blau
Trellick Tower, p015

Joakim Blockstrom
Dabbous, p055

Michael Bodiam
Café Royal, pp026-027

Theo Cook
Centre Point, p013
BT Tower, p014
Scott's, p050
St John Bread and
Wine, p054

Jason Hawkes
London city view,
inside front cover

Hufton + Crow
King's Cross Western
Concourse, pp068-069

Martin Jordan
Laban Building, p092

David Loftus
Brasserie Zédel, p056

Lee Mawdsley
David Gill Galleries, p073

Jamie McGregor Smith
Bulgari, p020, p021
ME, p028
19 Greek Street, p033
The Photographers'
Gallery, p037
Shrimpy's, p038, p039
Pizarro, p041
Pollen Street Social,
pp044-045
Experimental Cocktail
Club, p051
Tramshed, pp052-053
NOPI, pp058-059
Kirsty Carter, p063
New Court, p066
The Shard, p067
Late Night Chameleon
Cafe, pp074-075

Patricia Niven
St John Hotel, pp022-023

Dennis Gilbert/NTPL
The Homewood, pp100-101

Chris Parker
De La Warr Pavilion, p097

Simon Phipps
Economist Building, p065

Christoffer Rudquist
30 St Mary Axe, p012
40 Winks, p024
Claridge's, p025
Boundary, pp030-031
Dock Kitchen, pp042-043
Pizza East, p046
Polpo, p047
Dinner by
Heston, pp048-049
Morito, p057
L'Anima, p060
The Connaught Bar, p061
Barbican, p071
Jasper Morrison
Shop, p076
Labour and Wait, p077
Charlotte Olympia,
pp078-079
Hostem, p080
Liberty, p081
Darkroom, pp082-083
Dover Street
Market, p084
Mint, p085
Margaret Howell,
pp086-087
Dunhill, p089
Aman Spa at The
Connaught, pp094-095

Clare Skinner
Lord's, p093

Edmund Sumner
Velodrome, pp090-091

LONDON
A COLOUR-CODED GUIDE TO THE HOT 'HOODS

CENTRAL
The bustling commerce of the West End is leavened by Bloomsbury's cultured calm

NORTH
King's Cross might be arriving, but glorious, laidback Primrose Hill is already there

THE CITY
By day, the increasingly high-rise centre of the financial world; by night, largely deserted

SOUTH-WEST
If you're looking to snare a Russian oligarch or an Arab prince, start your search here

WEST
Stucco central, this is what first-time visitors expect to find everywhere in the city, sadly

WESTMINSTER
To dodge the coach-party crowds, get in, get a glimpse of the urban Gothic, then get out

EAST
The locus of London cool has been steadily shifting this way for more than a decade

SOUTH-EAST
One of the fastest-changing areas of London is heading upwards at a dizzying rate

For a full description of each neighbourhood, see the Introduction.
Featured venues are colour-coded, according to the district in which they are located.